The Lake District
Days amongst the Lakes and Hills

Front Cover: Evening on Buttermere

Photography by
Trevor Allen

Designed and Written by
Peter & Charlotte Hingston

Postcards: Some of the photographs in this book are available as postcards from Gallery Photography (Tel: 0553 810369).

Technical Note: The photographs were taken using mainly Hasselblad cameras with lenses from 50mm to 250mm and Fuji film.

Published 1991 jointly by Hingston Associates and Gallery Photography.

Distributor: Gallery Photography, School Road, Runcton Holme, King's Lynn, Norfolk PE33 0AN, England. Tel: 0553 810369 and Fax: 0553 810369.

Captions typeset in 10pt on I11.5 Symbol Bold and Medium.
Translations by: Pholiota Translations, 20-22 York Way, London N1 9AA.
Book printed and bound in Great Britain.

ISBN 0 906555 08 6

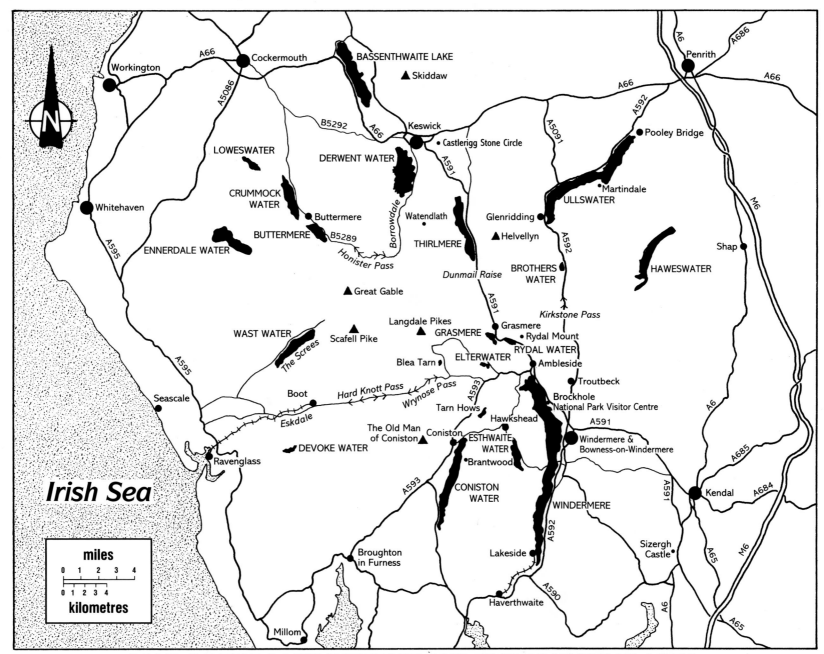

MAP OF THE LAKE DISTRICT AND SURROUNDING AREA

3

Start of a Beautiful Day A southern view along Derwent Water just before the sun catches the water. In the distance is Great Bay and the mouth of the River Derwent which flows through Borrowdale.

Icy Lake Ice borders Windermere on a wintery morning. Windermere is probably the Lake District's best known lake and it is the largest in England, being over 10 miles long and one mile wide. The word "mere" means "lake".

Lonely Sheep Solitude in Hard Knott Pass, the summit of which is at 394m (1,291ft).

(Left) **Cushion of Cloud** Grasmere hides under early morning cloud, as seen on the descent from Dunmail Raise.

(Overpage) **Hazy Morn** Early morning haze clears slowly from Grasmere.

Hidden Lake An early autumn view across Windermere to its western shore. It is the lake's peaceful side, with a lakeside public path and no major road. The distinctive peaks are the Langdale Pikes.

Misty Day Mist clings to Windermere's shoreline giving a sense of stillness and calm to this wintery scene. In the foreground is Ambleside, a mile north of Windermere and on the way to Rydal Water and Grasmere.

Storm Approaching Rain advancing up the Screes along the side of Wast Water. The Screes are nearly 600m (2,000ft) high and plunge to a depth of 79m (258ft). Wast Water is one of the most western lakes.

(Right) **Rising Mist** The green countryside near Hawkshead comes into view as the mist rises.

12

Reflections Rydal Water in autumnal colours. Grasmere and Rydal Water are linked by the River Rothay, which then flows south into Windermere. At Rydal Water's eastern end is Wordsworth's last home, Rydal Mount.

Rustic Calm Sheep grazing in Borrowdale. The hamlets of Seatoller, Stonethwaite, Borrowdale, Rosthwaite and Grange all lie in this dale. At the southern tip is Seathwaite where black lead (graphite) was mined for the world's first pencil factory, opened in Keswick in 1566.

Lakeland Town Ambleside in hazy sunshine. The town has less than 3,000 inhabitants but in the summer is crowded with visitors. Ambleside's most famous building is the picturesque "Bridge House", a tiny two-storey building on a small arched stone bridge over the stream Stock Beck. It is thought to have been built either as an apple-store or a summer house for nearby Ambleside Hall.

Rydal Mount Located between Ambleside and Rydal Water is Rydal Mount, the poet William Wordsworth's home from 1813 until his death in 1850. There are lovely views from the house and it is set in 4 acres of garden originally landscaped by Wordsworth. Even during his lifetime the house became a much visited shrine.

The Poet's Lake An idyllic day on Rydal Water. This small lake which is just ¾ mile long and ¼ mile wide is clearly visible from Rydal Mount. The fish beneath the waters are pike, perch and some brown trout.

Basking Yachts Moored yachts in White Cross Bay on Windermere. Overlooking the bay is Brockhole, the National Park's Visitor Centre. The Lake District became a National Park in 1951, and covers 880 square miles.

Sailing Afternoon A "Mirror" dinghy on Coniston Water. The lake has often been used for attempts on world water-speed records as it is over 5 miles long and very straight. It is where in 1959, Donald Campbell set a record of 260 mph in "Bluebird" and where he was sadly killed in another attempt in 1967.

Distant Outlook A north west view across Windermere, taken from near Gummer's How viewpoint. Many pleasure boats ply the lake, and among the best known are the three "steamers", the Swan, the Tern and the Teal. On the lakeside north of Bowness is the Windermere Steamboat Museum, housing a fine collection of vintage steamboats.

(Opposite)
Rolling Clouds and Rolling Hills
This is the northern half of Ullswater, seen from Martindale on the lake's quieter eastern side. The landscape here is gentle and rolling, but towards the southern end the mountains are grand and majestic. It is good walking country. Opposite this spot is Gowbarrow Park where Wordsworth saw the daffodils in his famous poem.

Rainbow Lake After the rain on Windermere. These are two of Windermere's many islands. Opposite Bowness is Belle Isle which at 38 acres is the largest island on the lake.

(Above) **Solitary Fisher** In several lakes, including Coniston, is found an ancient form of trout called "char", thought to have been trapped after the last Ice Age.

(Overpage) **Elterwater** And the Langdale Pikes.

Still Waters Peel Island and promontories reflected in Coniston Water. In the children's story "Swallows and Amazons" by Arthur Ransome, Wildcat Island was modelled on Peel Island.

Keswick View An expansive view of Derwent Water with a glimpse of Bassenthwaite Lake in the far distance. Keswick can be seen top right with Skiddaw rising to 931m (3,054ft) behind.

Ducks on Watendlath Beck Watendlath is a moorland hamlet of cottages and farm buildings above Borrow-dale. It is protected by the National Trust, and was the last place in the area to have mains electricity.

Dove Cottage This was William Wordsworth's home from 1799 to 1808. His sister, Dorothy, lived with him and while here he was married and three of his children were born. Next to the cottage is the Wordsworth Museum.

Boating Haven Waterhead is the northernmost pier for the Windermere steamers. Nearby are the remaining foundations of Galava Roman fort, best seen from the vantage point Todd Crag. It is thought to date from 79AD.

(Previous Page) At the Old Man's feet Coniston village lies at the base of the Old Man of Coniston, which rises to 801m (2,631ft).

High and Low The tip of England's highest mountain, Scafell Pike (977m, 3,206ft), looks over Wast Water, the deepest lake (79m, 258ft).

Great Gable Seen from the edge of Wast Water, this view is portrayed in the National Park's logo. On the left of Great Gable is Kirk Fell and Yewbarrow, and on its right is Lingmell Crag, and the start of the lakeside screes.

Lonely Splendour Glencoyne Farm, near the village of Glenridding on the south west side of Ullswater. The area is in a spectacular setting, surrounded by towering mountains, fells and pikes, with open easterly views over Ullswater. The word "fell" means "open hill slopes" and "pike" means "a sharply pointed summit".

(Opposite)
Blue Hills, Blue Lake This is picturesque Grasmere. On the eastern side of the lake is Dove Cottage, Wordsworth's home from 1799 to 1808. The house was originally an inn on the old pack-horse road.

Snow on the Fell Looking across Coniston Water from the north east. Coniston village was a mining centre until early this century, extracting copper in Coppermines Valley above the village. Slate quarries still operate.

Wordsworth's Birthplace The town of Cockermouth set against the Cumbrian hills. Fletcher Christian, the "Bounty" mutineer, was born here in 1764. In Main Street is the house where Wordsworth was born in 1770.

Glistening Waters Ullswater seen from Pooley Bridge. One of the Lake District's famous hotels, the Sharrow Bay, is located nearby. Just north of the village is the historic house of Dalemain. The house has parts which are medieval, Elizabethan and Georgian and its large garden contains rare trees and shrubs.

(Above) **Cool Waters** From its start near Wrynose Pass, the River Duddon flows south to the coast through Duddon Valley, known as Dunnerdale.

(Overpage) **Grasmere Reflected** The hill is Helm Crag and the saddle at the right is Dunmail Raise, through which the road passes from Grasmere to Thirlmere.

Blea Tarn Between the valleys of Great Langdale and Little Langdale is the ridge of Lingmoor Fell. A narrow road over the ridge links the two valleys and near the top is Blea Tarn. From that point are spectacular views including this one of the Langdale Pikes. "Blea Tarn" means "deep blue tarn" and three tarns in the Lake District have this name.

Tarn Hows Tarn Hows, off the Hawkshead to Coniston road, was originally three tarns. They were joined in the late 19th century with the building of a dam. The panoramic setting, wooded banks and path around it have made this the most visited of all lakes and tarns in the Lake District.

Rugged Volcanic Mountains In the valley of Borrowdale are the "Jaws of Borrowdale" where dramatically rugged hills close in to form a narrow passageway. This view is in upper Borrowdale, near Stonethwaite.

Soft Lighting This is Gatesgarth-dale Beck flowing down from Honister Pass to Buttermere and Crummock Water. The word "beck" means "stream". Long ago the two lakes of Crummock Water and Buttermere were one large lake. Gradual silting-up has divided them with three quarters of a mile of flat ground. The village of Buttermere lies between the two lakes.

(Opposite)
Bluebell Wood In dappled spring-time sunshine blooms a luxurious carpet of bluebells.

45

Watendlath Reflection Watendlath Tarn is owned by the National Trust. "Tarn" is the name given to the numerous small mountain lakes. The lakes and tarns were formed by the gouging action of Ice Age glaciers.

Water under the Bridge On the road to Watendlath, Ashness Bridge spans Ashness Gill which runs north into Derwent Water. Beyond are the peaks of Skiddaw and a glimpse of distant Bassenthwaite Lake.

Tranquillity High above this hamlet of Seatoller in Borrowdale is Honister Pass (358m, 1,176ft). Above the pass are tunnels to quarries of green volcanic slate, mined since the 1640s, and much used in local building.

(Previous Page)
Majestic Trees Derwent Water is the golden pool, with the houses of Keswick in the foreground. This is the town of Canon Rawnsley (1851-1920), who was a founder of the National Trust and an early Lake District preservationist. He encouraged Beatrix Potter to have her first book, "Peter Rabbit", published in 1895. She later bought Hill Top farm near Hawkshead.

Frozen Grandeur Winter seems to accentuate the rugged landscape here in Kirkstone Pass. The Lake District's dry stone walls, constructed without any form of mortar, were mostly made between the mid 18th and mid 19th centuries. They cross even the roughest, steepest terrain.

Wintery Light Herdwick and Swaledale are the main breeds of sheep in the Lake District. The woollen industry which sprung up was centred on Kendal until after the Industrial Revolution, when Carlisle rose in importance.

Sheep or Stones? The sheep seem to mimic the Castlerigg Stone Circle. The famous Circle located just east of Keswick is around 3,500 years old and comprises 38 stones in an oval ring of nearly 100 feet in diameter, the largest stone being over 7 feet tall.

(Opposite) **Peace and Quiet** A tranquil evening on Coniston Water. This is the lake where the National Trust runs the restored 1859 eighty-passenger steam yacht "Gondola".

Shades of Softness St Herbert's Island on Derwent Water waits in the twilight for nightfall. This island is said to have been the home of St Herbert, a disciple of St Cuthbert. Bassenthwaite Lake appears in the distance.

Silvery Sparkle Evening clouds roll towards Ullswater. To the lake's south- western end rises Helvellyn, which is 950m (3,116ft) in height. A local midsummer tradition is to climb the summit to see the sunrise.

(Opposite) **Purple Pool** A chilly evening sets in on the fells around Ullswater.

(Above) **Tranquil Evening** As dusk falls and the shadows lengthen, water ripples quietly against yachts on Windermere near Bowness. There has been a ferry across the lake from Bowness for c.500 years.

Canoes Come Ashore End of the day on Derwent Water. In winter this lake is one of the first to freeze over because its average depth is only 18 feet. Then it's skates, not canoes, one needs.

(Opposite)
Pastel Sunset A Windermere steamer puffs homewards along the lake. The top of Wray Castle can just be seen in the trees.

The Day Reflected Perfect peace and calm on Ullswater, looking southwards from near Pooley Bridge. A small jetty awaits the return of a boat.

Fiery Glow Ullswater at twilight, its water appearing like molten gold. The birds seem to rise for a better view.

Distant Sea A western view from Hard Knott Pass to the extremity of Cumbria and the Irish Sea beyond.
In the foreground is Eskdale through which runs England's oldest narrow-gauge steam railway.

Crescent Moon Last view of the day, from the summit of the Roman road between the forts at Galava (by Waterhead) and Glannaventa (by Ravenglass). Near here, in Hard Knott Pass, are the remains of another fort.

I wandered lonely as a cloud
That floats on high o'er vales and hills,
When all at once I saw a crowd,
A host of golden daffodils;
Beside the lake, beneath the trees,
Fluttering and dancing in the breeze.

Continuous as the stars that shine
And twinkle on the milky way,
They stretched in never-ending line
Along the margin of the bay;
Ten thousand saw I at a glance,
Tossing their heads in sprightly dance.

The waves beside them danced, but they
Out-did the sparkling waves in glee;
A poet could not but be gay,
In such a jocund company;
I gazed, and gazed, but little thought
What wealth the show to me had brought.

For oft, when on my couch I lie
In vacant or in pensive mood,
They flash upon that inward eye
Which is the bliss of solitude;
And then my heart with pleasure fills,
And dances with the daffodils.

William Wordsworth (1770-1850)

Wordsworth's famous Daffodils It was on the western side of Ullswater in Gowbarrow Park that William and his sister Dorothy were walking when they came across the daffodils which inspired this famous poem. According to Dorothy's journal the day was 15th April 1802.

(Back Cover) Kirkstone Pass Of the famous passes in the Lake District – Honister, Wrynose, Hard Knott and Kirkstone – Kirkstone is the highest at 454m (1,489ft). This view is looking north over Brothers Water.

Légende des photographies

En couverture Le soir sur Buttermere.

4   Début d'une belle journée Une vue vers le Sud sur Derwent Water juste avant que le soleil n'atteigne l'eau. Au loin, on aperçoit Great Bay et l'embouchure de la rivière Derwent qui traverse Borrowdale.

5   Lac glacé La glace entoure Windermere en ce matin d'hiver. Windermere, probablement le lac le plus connu du Lake District, est le plus grand en Angleterre, avec plus de 16 km de long et 1,6 km de large. Le mot *mere* signifie *lac*.

6   Coussin de nuages Grasmere se cache derrière les nuages de l'aube, sur cette vue prise en descendant de Dunmail Raise.

7   Moutons solitaires Solitude au col de Hard Knott Pass, dont le sommet culmine à 394 m.

8/9 Matin brumeux La brume du matin sur Grasmere se dissipe lentement.

10   Lac caché Une vue de Windermere jusqu'à sa rive Ouest, en début d'automne. C'est le côté paisible du lac, longé par un sentier et sans route principale. Les pics caractéristiques sont les Langdale Pikes.

11   Journée brumeuse La brume s'accroche aux rives du lac Windermere, donnant à cette scène hivernale une impression d'immobilité et de calme. Au premier plan, Ambleside, à environ 1 km au Nord de Windermere, en chemin pour Rydal Water et Grasmere.

12   Approche d'un orage La pluie se fraie un chemin sur les éboulis (screes) le long de Wast Water. Les Screes font presque 600 m de haut et plongent à une profondeur de 79 m. Wast Water est un des lacs les plus à l'Ouest.

13   Brume se dissipant La brume qui se dissipe révèle la campagne verdoyante, près de Hawkshead.

14   Reflets Rydal Water dans ses couleurs d'automne. Grasmere et Rydal Water sont reliés par la rivière Rothay, qui se déverse plus loin, au Sud, dans le lac Windermere. A l'extrémité Est de Rydal Water se dresse la dernière demeure de Wordsworth, Rydal Mount.

15   Calme campagnard Des moutons broutent à Borrowdale. Les hameaux de Seatoller, Stonethwaite, Borrowdale, Rosthwaite et Grange sont tous nichés dans cette vallée. A l'extrémité Sud se trouve Seathwaite, où autrefois, était extraite la mine de plomb pour la première usine de crayons à papier au monde, ouverte à Keswick en 1566.

16 (haut) Ville de la Région des Lacs Ambleside sous un soleil voilé. La ville a moins de 3 000 habitants, mais en été, elle fourmille de vacanciers. Le plus célèbre bâtiment de Ambleside est *Bridge House*, minuscule bâtisse de deux étages construite sur un petit pont de pierre qui enjambe le ruisseau Stock Beck. On pense qu'il a été construit pour servir d'entrepôt à pommes, ou faire office de maison d'été pour les propriétaires de Ambleside Hall, tout proche.

16 (bas) Rydal Mount Entre Ambleside et Rydal Water se trouve Rydal Mount, la maison du poète William Wordsworth de 1813 jusqu'à sa mort en 1850. La maison, entourée de 1,5 hectares de jardins aménagés à l'origine par Wordsworth, offre de très belles vues. Déjà durant la vie du poète, la maison était un lieu très visité.

17   Le lac du Poète Une journée idyllique sur Rydal Water. Ce petit lac, tout juste long de 1,2 km et large de 400 m, se voit très clairement de Rydal Mount. Dans ses eaux nagent des brochets, des perches et quelques truites de rivière.

18   Voiliers au soleil Voiliers amarrés à White Cross Bay sur Windermere. Brockhole, le Centre d'information du Parc National surplombe la baie. Le Lake District est devenu un Parc National en 1951, et couvre presque 250 000 hectares.

19   Après-midi de plaisance Un dériveur *Mirror* sur Coniston Water. Coniston a souvent été utilisé pour les tentatives de record mondial de vitesse sur l'eau, parce qu'il fait plus de 8 km de long et qu'il est très droit. C'est là qu'en 1959, Donald Campbell établit un record de vitesse de 418 km à l'heure sur *Bluebird*, et que malheureusement, il se tua lors d'un autre essai en 1967.

20   Vue dans le lointain Une vue du Nord-Ouest sur Windermere, prise près du point de vue de Gummer's How. De nombreux bateaux de plaisance parcourent le lac; parmi les plus connus figurent les trois *vapeurs*, le Swan, le Tern et le Teal. En bordure du lac, au Nord de Bowness, se trouve le Musée du Bateau à Vapeur de Windermere, qui abrite une belle collection de bateaux à vapeur anciens.

21   Collines ondulantes Voici la moitié Nord de Ullswater, vue de Martindale sur le côté Est, plus calme, du lac. Le paysage est ici doux et ondulant, mais vers l'extrémité Sud, les montagnes sont imposantes et majestueuses. C'est un endroit idéal pour la randonnée pédestre. En face de ce site, se trouve Gowbarrow Park, où Wordsworth vit les jonquilles de son célèbre poème.

22   Lac à l'arc-en-ciel Windermere après la pluie. Voici deux des plusieurs îles sur Windermere. La plus grande, Belle Isle, fait 15 hectares et partage presque le lac en deux, en face de Bowness.

23   Pêcheur solitaire Dans plusieurs lacs, dont Coniston, se trouve une ancienne espèce de truite, l'omble chevalier, qui en serait restée prisonnière après la dernière glaciation.

24/25 Elterwater Et les Langdale Pikes.

26   Eaux tranquilles L'île de Peel Island et ses promontoires se reflètent dans Coniston Water. Dans le livre pour enfants, *Swallows and Amazons* de Arthur Ransome, Wildcat Island est modelée sur Peel Island.

27   Vue sur Keswick Une vue panoramique sur Derwent Water. Au loin, on aperçoit le lac Bassenthwaite. La ville de Keswick se distingue en haut à droite, avec au fond, le mont Skiddaw qui culmine à 931 m.

28 Canards sur Watendlath Beck Watendlath est un hameau de cottages et bâtiments de ferme dans la lande au-dessus de Borrowdale. Il est protégé par le National Trust, et fut le dernier endroit de la région à être raccordé à l'électricité en 1978.

29 Dove Cottage Ce fut la première maison de William Wordsworth, entre 1799 et 1808. Sa soeur Dorothy y vivait avec lui, et c'est durant cette période qu'il se maria et que trois de ses enfants naquirent. Près du cottage se trouve le Musée Wordsworth.

30 Paradis de la plaisance Waterhead est l'embarcadère le plus au Nord utilisé par les vapeurs de Windermere. Tout près se trouvent les vestiges du fort romain de Galava, dont on a une vue excellente de Todd's Crag. Il daterait de 79 après J.-C.

31 Aux pieds du Vieil Homme Le village de Coniston est blotti au pied de la montagne Old Man of Coniston, qui s'élève à 801 m.

32 Deux extrêmes Le sommet de la plus haute montagne de l'Angleterre, Scafell Pike (977 m), surplombe Wast Water, le lac le plus profond (79 m).

33 Great Gable Cette vue prise de la rive de Wast Water figure sur le logo du Parc National. Sur la gauche de la montagne Great Gable se trouvent Kirk Fell et Yewbarrow, et sur la droite Lingmell Crag, et le début des éboulis sur les versants du lac.

34 Splendeur solitaire Voici Glencoyne Farm, près du village de Glenridding sur la rive Sud-Ouest de Ullswater. Le site est tout à fait spectaculaire, entouré de montagnes imposantes, de *fells* et de pics de presque tous les côtés, et offrant de larges vues vers l'Est sur Ullswater. Le mot *fell* signifie *larges versants de colline*.

35 Monts bleus, lac bleu Voici le pittoresque Grasmere. Du côté Est du lac se trouve Dove Cottage, la demeure de Wordsworth de 1799 à 1808. A l'origine, la maison était une auberge sur l'ancien sentier muletier.

36 Neige sur le mont Vue sur Coniston Water du Nord-Est. Le village de Coniston était un centre minier jusqu'au début du siècle; on y extrayait du cuivre dans la Coppermines Valley au-dessus du village. Les carrières d'ardoise sont encore en activité.

37 Lieu de naissance de Wordsworth La ville de Cockermouth se détachant sur les collines de Cumbria. Fletcher Christian, le mutin du *Bounty* y est né en 1764. Dans Main Street se trouve la maison où Wordsworth est né en 1770.

38 Eaux scintillantes Ullswater vu de Pooley Bridge. Un des hôtels les plus célèbres du Lake District, le Sharrow Bay, est situé non loin. Tout de suite au nord du village se trouve la demeure historique de Dalemain. Celle-ci comporte des parties médiévale, elizabéthaine et géorgienne, et son grand jardin contient plantes et arbres rares.

39 Eaux fraîches De sa source sur les monts désolés près de Wrynose Pass, la rivière Duddon oblique vers le Sud et coule jusqu'à la côte, traversant les paysages variés de la vallée Duddon, connue sous le nom de Dunnerdale.

40/41 Reflets sur Grasmere La haute colline est Helm Crag, et sur la droite de la photographie se dessine le col de Dunmail Raise, par où passe la route qui mène de Grasmere à Thirlmere.

42 (haut) Blea Tarn Entre les vallées de Great Langdale et Little Langdale se profile la crête de Lingmoor Fell (466 m). Sur le Fell, une route étroite relie les deux vallées, et au sommet se trouve Blea Tarn. Les vues y sont spectaculaires, comme celle-ci des Langdale Pikes. *Blea Tarn* signifie *lac bleu profond* et trois différents lacs du Lake District portent ce nom.

42 (bas) Tarn Hows Tarn Hows, sur la route entre Hawkshead et Coniston, était à l'origine formé de trois lacs. Ceux-ci furent reliés vers la fin du 19e siècle par la construction d'un barrage. Le site panoramique, les rives boisées et le sentier qui l'entoure en font le plus visité de tous les lacs et *tarns* du Lake District.

43 Monts volcaniques. Dans la vallée de Borrowdale se trouvent les *Jaws of Borrowdale* (Mâchoires de Borrowdale) où des monts aux contours déchiquetés se resserrent pour former un passage étroit. Cette vue est prise du haut de Borrowdale, près de Stonethwaite.

44 Jacinthes des bois Sous le soleil printanier fleurit un somptueux tapis de jacinthes des bois.

45 Lumière douce Voici Gatesgarthdale Beck, qui coule de Honister Pass à Buttermere et Crummock Water. Le mot *beck* signifie *ruisseau*. Il y a bien longtemps, les lacs de Buttermere et de Crummock Water ne formaient qu'un seul grand lac. L'envasement progressif les a séparé par 1 km de terrain plat. Le village de Buttermere est niché entre les deux lacs.

46 Reflets sur Watendlath Watendlath Tarn appartient au National Trust. *Tarn* est le nom donné aux nombreux petits lacs de montagne. Les lacs et tarns ont été façonnés par les glaciers de l'époque glaciaire.

47 Eau sous le pont Sur la route de Watendlath, Ashness Bridge enjambe Ashness Gill qui se jette au Nord dans Derwent Water. Dans le fond se dressent les pics de Skiddaw, et on aperçoit au loin le lac de Bassenthwaite.

48 Tranquillité Honister Pass (358 m) surplombe ce hameau de Seatoller dans Borrowdale. Au dessus du col, des tunnels mènent à des carrières d'ardoise volcanique verte, extraite depuis les années 1640, et très utilisée dans la construction locale.

49 Arbres majestueux Le lac de Derwent Water est la tache dorée, avec les maisons de Keswick au premier plan. Voici la ville du Chanoine Rawnsley (1851-1920), un des fondateurs du National Trust, et un des premiers défenseurs du Lake District. Il encouragea Beatrix Potter à faire publier son premier livre *L'histoire de Pierre le lapin*, en 1895. Celle-ci acheta plus tard la ferme de Hill Top, près de Hawkshead.

50 Grandeur glacée L'hiver semble accentuer l'âpreté du paysage, ici à Kirkstone Pass. Les murs de pierres sèches du Lake District, construits sans aucun mortier, ont été bâtis pour la plupart entre le milieu du 18e et le milieu du 19e siècle. Ils parcourent même les terrains les plus rudes et escarpés.

51 Lumière hivernale Herdwick et Swaledale sont les deux grandes races de mouton du Lake District. L'industrie de la laine était centrée à ses débuts autour de Kendal, jusque après la Révolution Industrielle qui vit l'essor de Carlisle.

52 Moutons ou pierres? Les moutons semblent imiter le Cercle de Pierre de Castlerigg. Le célèbre cercle, situé à l'Est de Keswick, a environ 3500 ans et comprend 38 pierres formant un ovale de près de 30 m de diamètre. La plus grande pierre mesure plus de 2 m de haut.

53 Calme parfait Le calme du soir sur Coniston water. C'est le lac sur lequel navigue *Gondola*, le yacht à vapeur restoré appartenant au National Trust. Il date de 1859, et peut embarquer 80 passagers.

54 Teintes douces Au crépuscule, l'île St Herbert sur Derwent Water attend la tombée de la nuit. On prétend que cette île a servi de demeure à Saint Herbert, un disciple de Saint Cuthbert. Le lac de Bassenthwaite se distingue dans le fond.

55 Eclat argenté Les nuages du soir avancent vers Ullswater. A l'extrémité Sud-Ouest du lac se dresse Helvellyn, la deuxième plus haute montagne d'Angleterre, avec 950 m. A la Saint-Jean, une tradition locale consiste à grimper jusqu'au sommet pour assister au lever du soleil.

56 Lac violet Un soir froid tombe sur les monts qui entourent Ullswater.

57 Soir paisible Tandis que point le crépuscule et que les ombres s'allongent, l'eau clapote doucement contre les yachts sur le lac Windermere, près de Bowness. Depuis près de 500 ans, un bac traverse le lac à partir de Bowness.

58 Des kayaks acostent Fin de journée sur Derwent Water. En hiver, ce lac est un des premiers à geler, parce que sa profondeur moyenne est de 5 m seulement. A la place des kayaks, les patins sont alors de rigueur.

59 Coucher de soleil pastel Un vapeur retourne vers la jetée sur Windermere. Le haut de Wray Castle se profile à travers les arbres.

60 Reflets d'une journée Un calme parfait sur Ullswater, avec cette vue vers le Sud prise près de Pooley Bridge. Une petite jetée attend le retour d'un bateau.

61 Incandescence Ullswater au crépuscule, ses eaux pareilles à de l'or fondu. Les oiseaux semblent voler plus haut pour jouir de la vue.

62 Mer lointaine Une vue vers l'Ouest de Hard Knott Pass jusqu'à l'extrémité du Cumbria, avec dans le fond, la Mer d'Irlande. Au premier plan, on aperçoit Eskdale, par où passe le plus ancien chemin de fer à voie étroite pour locomotives à vapeur en Angleterre.

63 Croissant de lune Dernière vue de la journée, du sommet de la route romaine entre les forts de Galava (par Waterhead) et de Glannaventa (par Ravenglass). Près d'ici, à Hard Knott Pass, se trouvent les ruines d'un autre fort.

Quatrième de couverture: Kirkstone Pass Culminant à 454 m, ce col est le plus haut des célèbres cols du Lake District, Honister, Wrynose, Hard Knott et Kirkstone. Voici une vue vers le Nord sur Brothers Water.

Texte français: Pholiota Translations, Londres.

Bildunterschriften

Titelphoto Abend auf dem Buttermere.

4 Ein schöner Tag beginnt Ein Blick über den Derwent Water gen Süden kurz bevor der erste Sonnenstrahl auf das Wasser fällt. Im Hintergrund sind die Great Bay und die Mündung des Flusses Derwent, der durch das Borrowdale fliesst, zu sehen.

5 Eis auf dem See Der eisbedeckte Windermere an einem Wintermorgen. Der Windermere ist vielleicht der bekannteste See des Lake Districts und darüber hinaus mit 16 Kilometern Länge und etwa einem Kilometer Breite der grösste See Englands. Das Wort *mere* bedeutet *See*.

6 Wolkenkissen Der Grasmere verbirgt sich an einem frühen Morgen hinter Wolken. Blick vom Dunmail Raise aus.

7 Einsames Schaf Abgeschiedenheit auf dem Hard Knott Pass, dessen Gipfel auf einer Höhe von 394 Metern liegt.

8/9 Diesiger Morgen Der frühe Morgendunst verzieht sich langsam über dem Grasmere.

10 Verborgener See Blick über den Windermere auf sein Westufer im Frühherbst. Dies ist die ruhigere Seite des Sees, es gibt keine grössere Strasse und ein Wanderpfad führt am Ufer entlang. Bei den markanten Berggipfeln handelt es sich um die Langdale Pikes.

11 Nebliger Tag Nebel hängt über den Ufern des Windermere und verleiht dieser winterlichen Szenerie Ruhe und Frieden. Im Vordergrund des Bildes ist das Dorf Ambleside zu sehen, das etwa einen Kilometer nördlich des Windermere auf dem Weg nach Rydal Water und Grasmere liegt.

12 Nahender Sturm Regenwolken brauen sich über den Abhängen entlang der Ufer des Wast Water zusammen. Diese Geröllablagerungen sind fast 600 M hoch und dehnen sich bis zu einer Breite von 79 M aus. Der Wast Water ist einer der westlichsten Seen.

13 Aufsteigender Nebel Unter den sich verziehenden Nebelschwaden kommt die grüne Landschaft in der Nähe von Hawkshead zum Vorschein.

14 Spiegelungen Der Rydal Water ist herbstlich eingefärbt. Der Grasmere und der Rydal Water sind miteinander durch den Fluss Rothay verbunden, der weiter südlich in den Windermere fliesst. Am Ostende des Rydal Water liegt Rydal Mount, der letzte Wohnort des englischen Dichters William Wordsworth.

15 Ländliche Ruhe Grasende Schafe im Tal Borrowdale. Die Dörfchen Seatoller, Stonethwaite, Borrowdale, Rosthwaite und Grange liegen alle in diesem Tal. An seinem Südende liegt Seathwaite, hier wurde schwarzes Blei (Graphit) für die erste Bleistiftfabrik der Welt abgebaut. Sie wurde 1566 in Keswick eröffnet.

16 (oben) Stadt im Lakeland Ambleside in fahlem Sonnenlicht. Die Stadt hat zwar weniger als 3000 Einwohner, ist aber im Sommer von Besuchern überlaufen. Amblesides berühmtestes Haus ist das malerische *Bridge House* (Brückenhaus), ein winziges zweistöckiges Haus auf einem kleinen steinernen Brückenbogen, der sich über den Fluss Stock Beck wölbt. Es wird vermutet, dass es entweder als Lagerhaus für Äpfel diente oder als Sommerhäuschen für die nahegelegene Ambleside Hall errichtet wurde.

16 (unten) Rydal Mount Das zwischen Ambleside und Rydal Water gelegene Anwesen Rydal Mount war von 1813 an bis zu seinem Tod 1850 der Wohnort des Dichters William Wordsworth. Vom Haus aus kann man einige herrliche Ausblicke geniessen. Es liegt in einem 1,5 Hektar grossen Park, dessen Anlage von Wordsworth selber entworfen wurde. Bereits zu Lebzeiten des Dichters wurde dieses Haus zu einem vielbesuchten Juwel.

17 Der See des Dichters Ein idyllischer Tag am Rydal Water. Dieser kleine See – er ist knapp 1,2 Kilometer lang und 400 Meter breit – ist von Rydal Mount aus gut zu sehen. In diesem See gibt es Barsche, Hechte und Forellen.

18 Segelboote im Sonnenschein Vor Anker liegende Segelboote in der White Cross Bay auf dem Windermere. Von Brockhole aus kann man die ganze Bucht überblicken. Hier ist das Informationszentrum des Nationalparks. Der Lake District wurde 1951 zum Nationalpark erklärt. Er bedeckt eine Fläche von fast 250.000 Hektar.

19 Segler am Nachmittag Ein Dingi des Typs *Mirror* auf dem Coniston Water. Der Coniston Water ist 8 Kilometer lang und schnurgerade. Er wird deshalb vielfach für Weltrekordversuche im Rennbootfahren benutzt. Hier erreichte Donald Campbell 1959 die Rekordgeschwindigkeit von 418 Km/Std mit seinem Boot *Bluebird*. Bei einem neuerlichen Rekordversuch kam er hier 1967 bei einem tragischen Unfall um's Leben.

20 Fernblick Blick über den Windermere in Richtung Nordwest, aufgenommen in der Nähe des Aussichtspunktes Gummer's How. Viele Vergnügungsdampfer kreuzen auf dem See. Die bekanntesten unter ihnen sind die Schiffe *Swan, Tern* und *Teal*. Am Seeufer nördlich von Bowness befindet sich Windermeres Dampfschifffahrtsmuseum, das eine hervorragende Sammlung von alten Dampfschiffen beherbergt.

21 Ziehende Wolken und sanfte Hügel Abgebildet ist die Nordhälfte des Ullswater, von Martindale aus gesehen, dem ruhigeren Ostufer des Sees. Die Landschaft ist sanft und hügelig, aber auf das südliche Ende zu finden sich grosse und majestätische Berge. Die Gegend ist ideal für Wanderungen. Diesem Aussichtspunkt gegenüber liegt der Gowbarrow Park, in dem Wordsworth jene Narzissen sah, die er in einem seiner berühmtesten Gedichte beschrieb.

22 Regenbogensee Nach einem Regenschauer auf dem Windermere. Zu sehen sind zwei der vielen Inseln des Windermere. Die grösste von ihnen ist die 15 Hektar grosse Insel Belle Isle. Sie teilt – gegenüber dem Ort Bowness gelegen – den See in zwei fast symmetrische Hälften.

23 Einsamer Fischer In einigen der Seen, so auch im Coniston Water, gibt es noch eine alte Fischart, den *char* (eine Art Saibling).

24/25 Das Dorf Elterwater Im Hintergrund die Langdale Pikes.

26 Stille Wasser Peel Island und einige Vorgebirge spiegeln sich im Coniston Water. Peel Island diente Arthur Ransome als Vorbild für die Insel *Wildcat Island*, die in seinem Kinderbuch *Der Kampf um die Insel* vorkommt.

27 Blick auf Keswick Weitläufiger Blick über den Derwent Water. In weiter Ferne lugt der Bassenthwaite Lake hervor. Oben rechts im Bild ist die Stadt Keswick zu sehen, über der sich der 931 M hohe Berg Skiddaw erhebt.

28 Enten auf dem Bach Watendlath Beck Watendlath ist ein in der Moorlandschaft über Borrowdale gelegener Weiler mit kleinen Häuschen und Gehöften. Er steht unter dem Schutz des National Trust und wurde als letzte Ortschaft dieser Gegend 1978 mit einer Stromleitung versorgt.

29 Dove Cottage Hier lebte William Wordsworth mit seiner Schwester Dorothy von 1799 bis 1808. Während seines Aufenthalts in Dove Cottage heiratete er und drei seiner Kinder kamen hier zur Welt. Neben dem Haus befindet sich das Wordsworth Museum.

30 Hafen mit Booten Waterhead ist die nördlichste Anlegestelle für die Dampfer auf dem Windermere. In der Nähe befinden sich die Grundmauern der römischen Befestigung Galava, die am besten vom Aussichtspunkt Todd's Crag aus zu sehen sind. Man nimmt an, dass sie aus dem Jahre 79 nach Christus stammen.

31 Am Fuss des *Old Man* Das Dorf Coniston liegt am Fuss des 801 M hohen *Old Man of Coniston*.

32 Hoch und Tief Der Gipfel von Englands höchstem Berg, dem 977 M hohen Scafell Pike, überschaut den Wast Water, Englands tiefsten See. Er ist 79 M tief.

33 Great Gable Dieses Panorama, vom Wast Water aus gesehen, ist im Emblem des Nationalparks wiedergegeben. Links des Great Gable liegen die Berge Kirk Fell und Yewbarrow und rechts davon der Lingmell Crag und der Anfang der am Seeufer liegenden Kiesdünen.

34 Abgeschiedene Pracht Glencoyne Farm liegt in der Nähe des Dorfes Glenridding an der Südwestseite des Ullswater. Die Ortschaft befindet sich in einer grandiosen Umgebung, eingerahmt von imposanten Bergen, Hügeln (den sogenannten *fells*) und spitzen Gipfeln (den *pikes*). Ein weiter Ausblick eröffnet sich gen Osten über den Ullswater.

35 Blaue Hügel, blauer See Zu sehen ist der malerische Grasmere. An der Ostseite des Sees steht Dove Cottage, in dem Wordsworth von 1799 bis 1808 lebte. Ursprünglich war das Haus ein Gasthof an der alten Packpferdstrasse.

36 Schnee auf einem Hügel Blick aus dem Nordosten über den Coniston Water. Das Dorf Coniston war bis zum Beginn dieses Jahrhunderts ein Bergbauzentrum. In dem über dem Dorf gelegenen Coppermine Valley (Kupferminental) wurde Kupfer abgebaut. Bis zum heutigen Tag wird noch Schiefer gebrochen.

37 Wordworths Geburtsort Die Stadt Cockermouth mit der Hügellandschaft von Cumbria im Hintergrund. Fletcher Christian, der Anführer der Meuterer auf der *Bounty*, wurde hier 1764 geboren. In der *Main Street* steht das Haus, in dem Wordsworth 1770 geboren wurde.

38 Glitzerndes Wasser Der Ullswater von Pooley Bridge aus gesehen. Das nahegelegene Sharrow Bay Hotel ist eines der berühmtesten Hotels im Lake District. Nördlich des Dorfes befindet sich das historische Haus von Dalemain. Das Haus ist in verschiedenen Baustilen errichtet, die ältesten Teile gehen auf das Mittelalter und die elisabethanische Zeit zurück. Der übrige Teil des Hauses ist im georgianischen Stil erbaut. In dem grossen Garten finden sich seltene Bäume und Sträucher.

39 Kühles Gewässer Von seiner Quelle in der öden Hügellandschaft in der Nähe des Wrynose Pass wendet sich der Fluss Duddon nach Süden und fliesst durch die abwechslungsreiche Szenerie des Tals Duddon Valley, das besser als Dunnerdale bekannt ist, zur Küste.

40/41 Spiegelungen im Grasmere Der markante Hügel ist der Helm Crag und der Bergsattel rechts im Bild ist der Dunmail Raise, über den die Strasse von Grasmere nach Thirlmere führt.

42 (oben) Blea Tarn Zwischen den Tälern von Great Langdale und Little Langdale erhebt sich die 466 M hohe Hügelkette Lingmoor Fell. Eine schmale Strasse über den Kamm verbindet die beiden Täler, auf ihm liegt der See Blea Tarn. Unter den spektakulären Ausblicken, die man von hier aus geniessen kann, ist auch der hier abgebildete auf die Langdale Pikes. *Blea Tarn* bedeutet *tiefer blauer Bergsee* und drei verschiedene *Tarns* im Lake District tragen diesen Namen.

42 (unten) Tarn Hows Der Tarn Hows, der an der Strasse von Coniston nach Hawkshead liegt, bestand ursprünglich aus drei Bergseen. Durch die Errichtung eines Damms im späten 19. Jahrhundert enstand ein grosser See. Holzbänke, von denen aus man das Panorama geniessen kann, und ein Rundweg um den See haben ihn zum meist besuchten aller Seen und Bergseen des Lake District gemacht.

43 Schroffes vulkanisches Gebirge Im Tal von Borrowdale sind die Jaws of Borrowdale (der Schlund von Borrowdale), eine von zerklüfteten Felsen dramatisch gestaltete enge Schlucht. Der hier abgebildete Blick bietet sich im oberen Borrowdale in der Nähe von Stonethwaite.

44 Hyazinthenwald Von den Strahlen der Frühlingssonne verwöhnt, blüht ein Hyazinthenteppich in üppiger Pracht.

45 Sanftes Licht Der Fluss Gatesgarthdale Beck fliesst vom Honister Pass zum Buttermere und zum Crummock Water herab. Das Wort *beck* bedeutet soviel wie *Fluss*. In längst vergangenen Zeiten bildeten die beiden Seen Buttermere und Crummock Water zusammen einen grossen See. Die allmählich eintretende Versandung teilte ihn dann in zwei Hälften. Die beiden Seen sind heute durch eine 1 Km breite Ebene getrennt. Das Dorf Buttermere liegt zwischen den beiden Seen.

46 Spiegelungen auf dem Watendlath Tarn Der Watendlath Tarn gehört dem National Trust. *Tarn* werden die zahlreichen kleinen Bergseen genannt. Die Seen und Tarns entstanden durch Aushöhlungen, die die Gletscher der letzten Eiszeit hinterliessen.

47 Wasser unter der Brücke Auf der Strasse nach Watendlath überspannt die Ashness Bridge den Fluss Ashness Gill, der weiter nördlich in den Derwent Water fliesst. Die dahinter zu sehenden Berggipfel sind die Gipfel des Skiddaw und in der Ferne lässt sich der Bassenthwaite Lake erahnen.

48 Stille Hoch über dem Flecken Seatoller im Borrowdale liegt der Honister Pass (358 M). Über dem Pass befinden sich Tunnel, die zu den Steinbrüchen führen, in denen seit ungefähr 1640 grüner Schiefer abgebaut wird, der viel zum Hausbau in dieser Gegend verwendet wird.

49 Majestätische Bäume Das goldene Gewässer im Bildhintergrund ist der Derwent Water, mit den Häusern von Keswick im Vordergrund. Keswick ist die Stadt des Domherrn Rawnsley (1851-1920), der ein Mitbegründer des National Trust war und sich schon früh für die Erhaltung des Lake Districts einsetzte. Er war es auch, der die Kinderbuchautorin Beatrix Potter dazu ermutigte, 1895 ihr erstes Buch *Die Geschichte von Peter Hase* zu veröffentlichen. Sie kaufte später die Hill Top Farm in der Nähe von Hawkshead.

50 Eisige Pracht Der Winter scheint das schroffe Landschaftsbild hier um den Kirkstone Pass noch zu akzentuieren. Die steinernen Feldbegrenzungsmauern des Lake District, aufgeschichtet ohne jede Art von Mörtel, wurden zum grössten Teil zwischen der Mitte des 18. und der des 19. Jahrhunderts errichtet. Sie ziehen sich auch noch durch die steilsten und zerklüftetsten Gegenden.

51 Winterliches Licht Herdwick und Swaledale sind die beliebtesten Schafrassen im Lake District. Die Wollverarbeitung, um Kendal konzentriert, nahm durch die Industrielle Revolution sprunghaft zu, infolge derer auch die Stadt Carlisle zunehmend an Bedeutung gewann.

52 Schafe oder Steine? Die Schafe scheinen den Steinkreis von Castlerigg nachzuahmen. Der berühmte Kreis liegt ein wenig östlich von Keswick und ist 3500 Jahre alt. Er besteht aus 38 Steinen, die in einem ovalen Ring mit einem Durchmesser von fast 30 M angeordnet sind. Der grösste Stein ist über zwei Meter hoch.

53 Ruhe und Frieden Ein ruhiger Abend auf dem Coniston Water. Auf diesem See betreibt der National Trust das restaurierte Dampfschiff *Gondola* aus dem Jahre 1859, das bis zu 80 Passagiere an Bord aufnehmen kann.

54 Weiche Schattierungen Die Insel St. Herbert's Island wartet in der Dämmerung auf das Hereinbrechen der Nacht. Die Insel soll Heimstatt des heiligen Herbert, einem Schüler Sankt Cuthberts gewesen sein. In der Ferne ist der Bassenthwaite Lake zu sehen.

55 Silberner Glanz Abendwolken über dem Ullswater. Am südwestlichen Ende des Sees erhebt sich der Helvellyn, der mit 950 M der zweithöchste Berg Englands ist. In der Gegend ist es Brauch, zur Sommersonnenwende den Gipfel zu erklimmen, um von dort aus den Sonnenaufgang zu betrachten.

56 Violetter See Ein kühler Abend senkt sich auf die Hügel um den Ullswater.

57 Friedvoller Abend Mit Beginn der Dämmerung, wenn die Schatten länger werden, brechen sich sanfte Wellen an den Booten in der Nähe von Bowness auf dem Windermere. Von Bowness aus gibt es seit ungefähr 500 Jahren eine Fährverbindung über den See.

58 Ruderboote legen an Ein Tag geht zu Ende auf dem Derwent Water. Im Winter ist dieser See aufgrund seiner geringen Tiefe – im Mittel nur 5 M – einer der ersten, der zufriert. Dann sind nicht mehr Ruderboote gefragt, sondern Schlittschuhe.

59 Sonnenuntergang in Pastell Ein Dampfer auf dem Windermere tuckert über den See heimwärts. Die Turmspitzen des Wray Castle können gerade noch über den Bäumen ausgemacht werden.

60 Ein gespiegelter Tag Vollkommene Ruhe und Frieden auf dem Ullswater, aus der Nähe von Pooley Bridge aus mit Blick nach Süden gesehen. Ein kleiner Landungssteg erwartet die Rückkehr eines Bootes.

61 Feuriger Glanz Das Wasser des Ullswater erweckt in der Dämmerung den Eindruck geschmolzenen Goldes. Die Vögel scheinen in die Höhe zu fliegen, um eine bessere Aussicht zu haben.

62 Das Meer in der Ferne Ein Blick gegen Westen vom Hard Knott Pass aus auf die Ausläufer der Hügellandschaft Cumbrias und die dahinter liegende Irische See. Im Vordergrund liegt das Tal Eskdale, durch das auf der ältesten Schmalspurtrasse Englands eine Dampflokomotive fährt.

63 Aufgehender Mond Die letzte Aussicht des Tages, vom höchsten Punkt der Römerstrasse aus aufgenommen, die von der Festung Galava (bei Waterhead) zur Festung Glannaventa (bei Ravenglass) führt. Ganz in der Nähe, auf dem Hard Knott Pass, finden sich die Überreste einer weiteren Befestigung.

Umschlagphoto auf der Rückseite: Kirkstone Pass Von den berühmten Gebirgspässen des Lake District – Honister, Wrynose, Hard Knott und Kirkstone – ist der Kirkstone Pass mit 454 M der höchste. Unser Blick geht nach Norden über den See Brothers Water.

Deutsche übersetzung: Pholiota Translations, London.

イングランドの湖水地方